First Workshop on Corpus Generation and Corpus Augmentation for Machine Translation

AA005155

Held at AMTA 2022

Orlando, Florida, USA
12-16 September 2022

ISBN: 978-1-7138-6759-3

Printed from e-media with permission by:

Curran Associates, Inc.
57 Morehouse Lane
Red Hook, NY 12571

Some format issues inherent in the e-media version may also appear in this print version.

Copyright© (2022) by the Association for Computational Linguistics
All rights reserved.
Copyright for individual papers remains with the authors and are licensed under a Creative Commons 4.0 license, CC-BY-ND. (https://creativecommons.org/licenses/by-nd/4.0/)

Printed with permission by Curran Associates, Inc. (2023)

For permission requests, please contact the Association for Computational Linguistics at the address below.

Association for Computational Linguistics
209 N. Eighth Street
Stroudsburg, Pennsylvania 18360

Phone: 1-570-476-8006
Fax: 1-570-476-0860

acl@aclweb.org

Additional copies of this publication are available from:

Curran Associates, Inc.
57 Morehouse Lane
Red Hook, NY 12571 USA
Phone: 845-758-0400
Fax: 845-758-2633
Email: curran@proceedings.com
Web: www.proceedings.com

AMTA ORLANDO 2022

The 15th Conference of the Association for Machine Translation in the Americas

2022.amtaweb.org

PROCEEDINGS

Workshop on Corpus Generation and Corpus Augmentation for Machine Translation

Organizer: John E. Ortega

©2022 The Authors. These articles are licensed under a Creative Commons 4.0 license, no derivative works, attribution, CC-BY-ND.

Introduction to the First Workshop on Corpus Generation and Corpus Augmentation for Machine Translation (CoCo4MT) at the AMTA 2022 Conference

Organizers

John E. Ortega[1,2] john.ortega@usc.es
Marine Carpuat[3] marine@umd.edu
William Chen[4] williamchen@cmu.edu
Katharina Kann[5] katharina.kann@colorado.edu
Constantine Lignos[6] lignos@brandeis.edu
Maja Popopvić[7] maja.popovic@adaptcentre.ie
Shabnam Tafreshi[3] stafresh@umd.edu

[1]New York University
[2]University of Santiago de Compostela - CITIUS
[3]University of Maryland
[4]Carnegie Mellon University
[5]University of Colorado Boulder
[6]Brandeis University
[7]ADAPT Centre

1 Aim of the workshop

The first workshop on corpus generation and corpus augmentation for machine translation (CoCo4MT) sets out to be an original workshop centered around research that focuses on corpora creation, cleansing, and augmentation techniques specifically for machine translation.

We hope that submissions will provide high-quality corpora that is available publicly for download and can be used to increase machine translation performance thus encouraging new dataset creation for multiple languages that will, in turn, provide a general workshop to consult for corpora needs in the future.

2 Workshop scope and details

It is a well-known fact that machine translation systems, especially those that use deep learning, require massive amounts of data. Several resources for languages are not available in their human-created format. Some of the types of resources available are monolingual, multilingual, translation memories, and lexicons. Those types of resources are generally created for formal purposes such as parliamentary collections when parallel and more informal situations when monolingual. The quality and abundance of resources including corpora used for formal reasons is generally higher than those used for informal purposes. Additionally, corpora for low-resource languages, languages with less digital resources available, tends to be less abundant and of lower quality.

CoCo4MT sets out to be the first workshop centered around research that focuses on corpora creation, cleansing, and augmentation techniques specifically for machine translation. We accept work that covers any spoken language (including high-resource languages) but we are specifically interested in those submissions that are on languages with limited existing resources (low-resource languages) where resources are not highly available. Since techniques from high-resource languages are generally statistical in nature and could be used as generic solutions for any language, we welcome submissions on high-resource languages also.

The goal of this workshop is to begin to close the gap between corpora available for low-resource translation systems and promote high-quality data for online systems that can be used by native speakers of low-resource languages is of particular interest. Therefore, It will be beneficial if the techniques presented in research papers include their impact on the quality of MT output and how they can be used in the real world.

CoCo4MT aims to encourage research on new and undiscovered techniques. We hope that submissions will provide high-quality corpora that is available publicly for download and can be used to increase machine translation performance thus encouraging new dataset creation for multiple languages that will, in turn, provide a general workshop to consult for corpora needs in the future. The workshop's success will be measured by the following key performance indicators:

- Promotes the ongoing increase in quality of machine translation systems when measured by standard measurements,
- Provides a meeting place for collaboration from several research areas to increase the availability of commonly used corpora and new corpora,
- Drives innovation to address the need for higher quality and abundance of low-resource language data.

Please feel free to review the official workshop website: `https://sites.google.com/view/coco4mt` for more information and details.

3 Invited Speakers (listed alphabetically by first name)

We are happy our dear colleagues Ankur Parikh, Jörg Tiedemann, Julia Kreutzer, Graham Neubig, and Maria Nadejde have prepared talks on five important topics for CoCo4MT 2022.

3.1 Ankur Parikh, Google Research

Ankur Parikh is a staff research scientist at Google NYC. His research interests are in natural language processing and machine learning with a recent focus on high precision text generation. Ankur received his PhD from Carnegie Mellon in 2015 and has received a best paper runner up award at EMNLP 2014 and a best paper in translational bioinformatics at ISMB 2011.

3.2 Graham Neubig, Carnegie Mellon University

Graham Neubig is an associate professor at the Language Technologies Institute of Carnegie Mellon University. His research focuses on multilingual natural language processing, natural language interfaces to computers, and machine learning methods for NLP, with the final goal of every person in the world being able to communicate with each-other, and with computers in their own language. He also contributes to making NLP research more accessible through open publishing of research papers, advanced NLP course materials and video lectures, and open-source software, all of which are available on his web site.

3.3 Jörg Tiedemann, University of Helsinki

Jörg Tiedemann is professor of language technology at the Department of Digital Humanities at the University of Helsinki. He received his PhD in computational linguistics for work on bitext alignment and machine translation from Uppsala University before moving to the University of Groningen for 5 years of post-doctoral research on question answering and information extraction. His main research interests are connected with massively multilingual data sets and data-driven natural language processing and he currently runs an ERC-funded project on representation learning and natural language understanding.

3.4 Julia Kreutzer, Google Research

Julia is a research scientist at Google Research, Montreal, where she works on improving machine translation. She is generally interested in the intersection of natural language processing (NLP) and machine learning. In her PhD (Heidelberg University, Germany) she investigated how reinforcement learning algorithms can be used to turn weak supervision signals from users into meaningful updates for a machine translation system.

3.5 Maria Nadejde, Amazon

Maria is a Senior Applied Scientist at Amazon AWS AI working on improving quality and customization of Amazon Translate. Before joining Amazon, Maria was an Applied Research Scientist at Grammarly developing deep learning applications that enhance written communication. She obtained a PhD in Informatics from the University of Edinburgh on the topic of syntax-augmented machine translation.

3.6 Other speakers and guests

CoCo4MT decided to create a panel that includes several other researchers and notable speakers in order to provide collaboration amongst those wanting to assist with low-resource language approaches for corpora augmentation and generation. These speakers are to be announced in future (post-edited) version of the proceedings.

4 Program Committee (listed alphabetically by first name)

- Amirhossein Tebbifakhr, University of Trento
- Anna Currey, Amazon
- Ayush Singh, Northeastern University
- Barry Haddow, University of Edinburgh
- Bharathi Raja Chakravarthi, National University of Ireland Galway
- Beatrice Savoldi, University of Trento
- Constantine Lignos, Brandeis University
- Eleftheria Briakou, University of Maryland
- David Adelani, Saarland University
- Jasper Kyle Catapang, University of Birmingham
- John E. Ortega, University of Santiago de Compostela - CITIUS
- Jonathan Washington, Swarthmore College

- Jonne Sälevä, Brandeis University
- José Ramom Pichel Campo, University of Santiago de Compostela - CITIUS
- Katharina Kann, University of Colorado Boulder
- Kochiro Watanabe, The University of Tokyo
- Liangyou Li, Huawei
- Maja Popopvić, ADAPT Centre
- Maria Art Antonette Clariño, University of the Philippines Los Baños
- Marine Carpuat, University of Maryland
- Pablo Gamallo, University of Santiago de Compostela - CITIUS
- Patrick Simianer, Lilt
- Rico Sennrich, University of Zurich
- Rodolfo Joel Zevallos Salazar, Universitat Pompeu Fabra
- Shabnam Tafreshi, University of Maryland
- Shantipriya Parida, Idiap Research Institute
- Surafel Melaku Lakew, Amazon
- William Chen, Carnegie Mellon University
- Xing Niu, Amazon

Contents

English-Russian Data Augmentation for Neural Machine Translation

Nikita Teslenko Grygoryev n.grygoryev@pangeanic.com
Pangeanic BI Europa, S.L., Valencia, Spain
Mercedes García Martínez m.garcia@pangeanic.com
Pangeanic BI Europa, S.L., Valencia, Spain
Francisco Casacuberta Nolla fcn@prhlt.upv.es
Universitat Politècnica de València, Valencia, Spain
Amando Estela Pastor a.estela@pangeanic.com
Pangeanic BI Europa, S.L., Valencia, Spain
Manuel Herranz m.herranz@pangeanic.com
Pangeanic BI Europa, S.L., Valencia, Spain

Abstract

Data Augmentation (DA) refers to strategies for increasing the diversity of training examples without explicitly collecting new data manually. We have used neural networks and linguistic resources for the automatic generation of text in Russian. The system generates new texts using information from embeddings trained with a huge amount of data in neural language models. Data from the public domain have been used for experiments. The generation of these texts increases the corpus used to train models for NLP tasks, such as machine translation. Finally, an analysis of the results obtained evaluating the quality of generated texts has been carried out and those texts have been added to the training process of Neural Machine Translation (NMT) models. In order to evaluate the quality of the NMT models, firstly, these models have been compared performing a quantitative analysis by means of several standard automatic metrics used in machine translation, and measuring the time spent and the amount of text generated for a good use in the language industry. Secondly, NMT models have been compared through a qualitative analysis, where generated examples of translation have been exposed and compared with each other. Using our DA method, we achieve better results than a baseline model by fine tuning NMT systems with the newly generated datasets.

1 Introduction

The use of large, quality datasets to train neural network models for specific NLP tasks such as machine translation (MT), summarization, paraphrasing, text generation or dialogue systems is essential to achieve good quality results. Data augmentation (DA) has recently seen increased interest in Natural Language Processing (NLP) due to the lack of data in low-resource domains or new NLP tasks, and the popularity of large-scale neural networks that require large amounts of training data. Despite this recent upsurge, this area is still relatively underexplored. Perhaps this is due to the challenges posed by the discrete nature of language data which makes it challenging to make significant DA.

Although current progress in the areas of NLP and MT allows for the analysis, understanding, and automatic generation of increasingly accurate and fluid text, such amounts of data with good quality are hard to find. Sometimes, they are too scarce for use during the training of a neural network model.

These techniques are often investigated in Computer Vision (Perez and Wang, 2017) and DA's adaptation for NLP seems secondary and comparatively underexplored, especially in MT task.

There are several works that have been done previously such as (Fadaee et al., 2017) which is a data augmentation approach that targets low-frequency words by generating new sentence pairs containing rare words in new, synthetically created contexts; and (Sánchez-Cartagena et al., 2021) which present a multi-task DA approach in which they generate new sentence pairs with transformations, such as reversing the order of the target sentence, which produce unfluent target sentences. During training, these augmented sentences are used as auxiliary tasks in a multi-task framework with the aim of providing new contexts where the target prefix is not informative enough to predict the next word.

In this work we introduce a new DA technique based on words substitution of a specific type (noun, adjective or adverb) in a sentence using a language model (LM) which generates a new word according to the context of the sentence. In addition, we check the new generated word, in order to maintain the main quality of the sentence.

In the rest of this paper, our DA approach is presented in Section 3, Section 4 shows the results of the experiments, and Section 5 outlines our conclusions and proposals for future work.

2 Background

We present how neural machine translation models can translate sentences and how neural language models can generate new words. Moreover, we explain some state-of-the-art data augmentation techniques for text.

2.1 Neural Machine Translation

NMT aims to estimate an unknown conditional distribution $P(\mathbf{y}|\mathbf{x})$ where $\mathbf{x}$ and $\mathbf{y}$ are random variables that represent the source (input) and target (output) sentences (Bahdanau et al., 2015).

We assume that the input sentence is $\mathbf{x} = (x_1, \ldots, x_S)$ and the output sentence is $\mathbf{y} = (y_1, \ldots, y_T)$, S corresponds to the total number of input words and T to the total number of output words. Using the chain rule, the conditional distribution could be described as Equation 1.

$$\hat{\mathbf{y}}_1^{\hat{T}} = \arg\max_{T,\mathbf{y}_1^T} \prod_{t=1}^{T} Pr_\theta(y_t|y_1^{t-1}, c(x_1^S)) \tag{1}$$

where y_t represents the current translated word, which is generated from the previous translated words y_1^{t-1} using a type of representation denoted by c function of the input sentence $\mathbf{x}_1^S$ and using the parameters of the model θ estimated from a training dataset D.

Training is performed on a parallel corpus with stochastic gradient descent. For translation, a beam search with 5-10 size range is employed.

The Transformer (Vaswani et al., 2017) is the state-of-the-art architecture in NMT that aims to solve sequence-to-sequence tasks while handling long-range dependencies with ease. It relies entirely on self-attention to compute representations of its input and output without using sequence-aligned Recurrent Neural Networks (RNNs).

2.2 Language models based on Transformer architecture

Nowadays, for most NLP tasks aimed at encoding text sequences, language models based on Transformer architecture are the state-of-the-art. In addition, these models can be specialized in a specific task by fine-tuning the weights on a different task than the one they have been trained for. For that, the models are trained using supervised labelled data obtaining the best results until now. This methodology, where a model is first pre-trained and then specialized in a specific task, is called transfer learning. One of the first language models to use Transformer architecture is *Bidirectional Encoder Representations from Transformers* (BERT) (Devlin et al., 2019) that is based on the encoder of the Transformer. Then, *Robustly optimized BERT approach (RoBERTa)* (Zhuang et al., 2021) was developed which deletes the *Next Sentence Prediction* task, which is one of the objective functions that is used for training BERT and modifies the second objective function defined as the *Masked Language Model* by applying a dynamic approach instead of a static one. In addition, *Generative Pre-trained Transformer* (GPT) with its latest release GPT-3 (Floridi and Chiriatti, 2020) (Brown et al., 2020) was developed, which is formed of multiple Transformer decoder layers. For instance, the development of XLNet (Yang et al., 2019) brought a new approach by combining auto-regression, such as GPT-2 does, and found an alternative way to introduce bidirectional context as BERT or other similar architectures.

2.3 Data Augmentation

DA encompasses methods of increasing the size of training data without the necessity of manually collecting more data. Most strategies either add slightly modified copies of existing data or create synthetic data, aiming for the augmented data to act as a regularizer and reduce over-fitting when training machine learning models. The most popular technique of DA in NLP is Back-translation (Sennrich et al., 2016) which is used to generate parallel synthetic data starting from a monolingual corpus. Another technique is the substitution of words using pre-trained language modeling (Kumar et al., 2020). Also, Easy Data Augmentation (EDA) (Wei and Zou, 2019), which consists of four simple techniques (synonym replacement, random insertion, random swap and random deletion) that produce small changes in the original text, has been demonstrated to be as useful as other more complicated methods of DA.

In this work we present a more precise approach of substitution of words by word type and using pre-trained language modeling and POS-tagging, where we care about the quality, coherence and variety of new generated sentences. This approach is hypothetically more precise and accurate than other DA techniques presented earlier in this paper such as EDA techniques or back-translation, typically used for the generation of synthetic texts. Therefore, we aim to create not only a bigger but also a more diverse and domain-orientated training dataset.

3 Automatic generation of a parallel English-Russian corpus

In this section, we present our approach of generating a synthetic corpus in Russian using a pre-trained language model specialized in Russian called ruRoBERTa-large. This model performed better than the multilingual BERT language model in preliminary experiments.

The United Nations dataset (UN) (Ziemski et al., 2016) dataset for English to Russian version 1 has been used. We apply a cleaning process which consists in filtering out sentences that

- are shorter than 5 words because they are no relevant.
- are longer than 50 words in order to fit the maximum capacity of tokens in ruRoberta encoder.
- have Latin characters in the Russian side.
- have more punctuation marks than characters.
- have more than 10 words in the absolute difference comparing source and target sentence length.

- have more numbers than letters, both in Cyrillic and Latin alphabets.

After this cleaning process, we save 1 million sentences for DA application, 7.9 million sentences for baseline model training, 2000 sentences for validation and 2000 sentences for test.

We use a Part-Of-Speech tagger in order to select the type of word that is generated by the pre-trained LM. For that purpose, we have used a model called $ru\_core\_news\_lg$ trained with the Spacy (Honnibal and Montani, 2017) toolkit. This model determines if the type of the selected word (noun, adjective or adverb) to be changed is the same as the generated one, which guaranties a similar level of quality from the original sentence. In addition, we have used the Python library *pymorphy2*, which provides us the gender, person and number of the selected word. It also provides a lot of useful morphological information about the words which may be used for another data augmentation methods, like verbs substitution where the grammatical time is relevant.

During the empirical experimentation, we observed that the language model returns a score of the pertinence of generated word to the bidirectional context of the sentence. With this in mind, we established an acceptance threshold for each generated word, which is set to 0.07. This also reduces significantly the selection of useless and not significant words like one character words or punctuation marks. Thus, we can make a more precise and accurate word substitution by the generation of the new sentences in Russian. In the last step, we generate by high quality Pangeanic MT model the English part of the new sentences to obtain parallel corpus. Finally, we have created four completely new datasets which have been generated by four different methods: (1) substitution of adverbs, (2) substitution of nouns, (3) substitution of adjectives and (4) a mixture of the three methods where the selection of the methods is done equitably.

For basic methods (noun, adverbs and adjectives substitution) we select all the words of the selected type from the sentence using the POS-tagger and save the position of that words in the sentence, next we iterate over all the saved words, so in each iteration we took one word, save its gender and number using the *pymorphy2* library and change that word for the <MASK> token so the ruRoberta-large model can predict a new word which is evaluated by checking that the generated word

- is not the same word than original one.
- is not a useless word such as punctuation marks or prepositions.
- is the same in terms of gender and number than original one.

So when we haven't more words to be changed from the current sentence, we firstly check if at least one of the selected words have changed and if not we discard the sentence. Then, we select the next sentence to be augmented and repeat the process until there are no sentences left.

For the mix method we add an additional step before the selection of all the words of a specific type in a sentence. This step consists in selecting which method will be applied for the following sentence. This previous selection is done in a way that the final corpus has similar amount of new texts of each DA method used.

For all the methods, we stop when there is not more original sentences to be augmented.

Table 1 presents the number of new number of words, sentences and the mean of new words per sentence per method showing the number of computing days.

As we can see in Table 1, substitution of nouns is the method that produces the largest amount of words, sentences and gives the highest mean of words per sentence. This is due to Russian has a very rich vocabulary, especially when it comes to nouns and it is relatively easy to find an appropriate or accurate new noun that can fit in the context of the sentence.

Likewise, the adjectives and mix methods have also generated a significant amount of data. As nouns method substitution, adjectives are also a very heterogeneous and permissive when it

Method	New #words	New #sentences	New #words/sentence	Comp. days
Adverbs	275K	327K	1.2	5
Nouns	4.8M	922K	5.2	8
Adjectives	2.2M	800K	2.7	6
Mix	2M	504K	4	11

Table 1: Statistics of adverbs, nouns, adjectives and mixed substitution methods where the original number of sentences (1 million), generated new number of words, generated new number of sentences, mean of generated new words per sentence and the time used for each DA method using parallelized in 10 CPUs.

comes to substitution of another adjective that fits in the context of the sentence. As we can see, the mixed method combines the two most generative methods. This is because the mix method generates almost the same amount of data substituting the three types of words. The method that produces the least amount of data is adverbs because adverbs have less options of substitution. However, it took less time (5 days) than the rest of the methods.

Although the adjective method generated a similar amount of new sentences as nouns, its mean of words per sentences is the smallest of all four methods. Due to the number of adjectives in a sentence is significantly less than nouns.

By contrast, the mixed method generated fewer sentences than the nouns or adjectives methods, but has a significantly high mean of words per sentence. Although this method generates a dataset with high variety because of the combination of the type of words, it takes more time to compute due to the equality of the generation of type of words.

4 Experiments

Experiments have been performed in order to study how our DA method for a English-Russian dataset can improve NMT models.

The architecture of the machine translation models used is composed of 6 layers of encoder and 6 layers of decoder with 8 multihead attention units in both of them. This configuration is the same as the standard Transformer architecture.

On other hand, the maximum length of input and output sentences was established to 400 and batch size was set to 4096 tokens. For baseline model, we trained the model with 7.9 million samples of parallel data in 100000 training steps and for each model trained with extra data, we retrain the baseline model with an extra 50000 train steps using for each retrained model the data reflected in the Table 2. For each training process we have used the first 8000 steps for warm up, NOAM as a decay method and SGD as the optimizer method with $\epsilon = 0.05$. We have trained this model using the OpenNMT-py framework.

ONU dataset[1]		# Samples
Train	Original	7.9M
	Adverbs	271K
	Nouns	916K
	Adjectives	792K
	Mix	501K
Validation		2K
Test		2K

Table 2: Statistics of generated and original datasets.

As we can see in Table 2, after the cleaning process, we split the remaining of the original UN dataset for DA techniques, train, validation and test. For baseline models training set we picked 7.9 million samples. For DA techniques, we got 1 million samples which generated data used for the retraining of baseline models. Then, we save 2000 samples for validation set. Finally, we picked 2000 samples for testing set of the models.

4.1 Quantitative analysis

We have performed a quantitative analysis, for both Russian-English and English-Russian models, by comparing the corresponding baseline NMT model with the corresponding four methods trained with augmented data.

Therefore, six automatic evaluation metrics have been selected to automatically measure the NMT outputs: (1) *BiLingual Evaluation Understudy* (BLEU) (Papineni et al., 2002) which is the standard score used in machine translation evaluation, (2) *Translation Error Rate* (TER) (Snover et al., 2006) which looks for the total amount of edits needed to get the reference sentence from the hypothesis sentence, (3) ChrF-2 (Popović, 2015), which is the F-2 score but at char level, (4) NIST (Doddington, 2002), similar to BLEU but also calculates how informative a particular n-gram is, (5) *Better Evaluation as Ranking* (BEER) (Stanojević and Sima'an, 2014), which is a sentence level metric that can incorporate a large number of features combined in a linear model and (6) *Crosslingual Optimized Metric for Evaluation of Translation* (COMET) (Rei et al., 2020), which uses multilingual sentence embedding and the source sentence. The main goal of using a larger quantity of evaluation metrics than usual is to get a more precise information of the quality of the translations done by the NMT models.

Method	BLEU	TER	ChrF-2	NIST	BEER	COMET
Baseline	59.6 ± 1.4	31.4 ± 1.1	78.3	2.9	.73	.89
Adverbs	70.2 ± 1.4	21.4 ± 1.0	84.6	3.2	.79	.97
Nouns	68.8 ± 1.4	21.6 ± 1.0	83.9	3.2	.80	1
Adjectives	69.2 ± 1.4	22.1 ± 1.0	83.8	3.2	.79	.98
Mix	$\mathbf{70.9 \pm 1.3}$	$\mathbf{20.5 \pm 1.0}$	84.8	3.2	.80	1

Table 3: Results of the DA methods used (substitution of adverbs, nouns, adjectives and mix) applying a set of automatic evaluation metrics for machine translation models in English to Russian language direction. From left to right are BLEU, TER, ChrF-2, NIST, BEER and COMET. The value that follows the symbol $\pm$ is the confidence interval calculated using the bootstrap resampling technique.

The evaluation of models that were trained in the English-Russian direction is presented in Table 3. All DA substitution methods perform better compared to the NMT model in all the evaluation metrics. The mixed substitution method yields the best results of all the automatic evaluation metrics that have been calculated. As we can see in Table 3, we obtain a good scores when evaluating with COMET our models with augmented data where each one of them outperforms the baseline model.

This fulfills the hypothesis that a richer and more diverse dataset make translation models more accurate and which produces a more fluent translations.

However, as we can see in Table 4, best results were produced by the adjectives substitution method. Nevertheless, if we focus on the values of BLEU and TER and their confidence intervals, we can see that the values of the adjective and mixed substitution methods are similar. Therefore, we can deduce that mixed substitution method is also useful and produces good results. Furthermore, in both language directions (Russian to English and English to Russian) all the models that were retrained with augmented data perform better than the baseline model.

Method	BLEU	TER	ChrF-2	NIST	BEER	COMET
Baseline	40.9 ± 1.1	46.4 ± 1.1	62.3	2.6	.62	.28
Adverbs	47.1 ± 1.3	42.7 ± 1.1	71.9	2.7	.66	.25
Nouns	48 ± 1.2	43.1 ± 1.1	72.6	2.7	.67	.25
Adjectives	**48.3 ± 1.3**	**41.8 ± 1.1**	72.7	2.7	.67	.29
Mix	48 ± 1.3	42.5 ± 1.1	72.7	2.7	.68	.27

Table 4: Results of the DA methods used (substitution of adverbs, nouns, adjectives and mix) applying a set of automatic evaluation metrics for machine translation models in the Russian to English language direction. From left to right are BLEU, TER, ChrF-2, NIST, BEER and COMET. The value that follows the symbol ± is the confidence interval calculated using the bootstrap resampling technique.

Finally, as we can see in Table 4, the COMET values obtained using NMT models retrained with augmented data produce worse values but they are not statistically significant compared with the NMT baseline model. This is due to the fact that target (English) is synthetically generated using MT.

4.2 Qualitative analysis

We have randomly selected an example of the English to Russian models. The qualitative analysis showing the source sentence in English, the Russian translation reference and the machine translation sentences that have been generated by the NMT models are represented in Table 5. We can see the differences between the reference sentence and the different translations generated by the NMT models. The underlined words refer to the differences between each translation model. As we can see, the mixed method has more variability in the translation but keeps the overall meaning of the reference.

Method	Translations from English to Russian
Source	Their case also attracted the attention of the control commission in Geneva.
Reference	Их случай также привлек внимание комиссии по контролю в Женеве.
Baseline	Их дело также привлекло внимание комиссии по контролю в Женеве.
Adverbs	Их случай также привлек внимание контрольной комиссии в Женеве.
Nouns	Их дело также привлекло внимание комиссии по контролю в Женеве.
Adjectives	Их дело также привлекло внимание комиссии по контролю в Женеве.
Mix	Их дело также привлекло внимание контрольной комиссии в Женеве.

Table 5: Examples of translations obtained when translating using the models trained with the datasets generated using substitution of adverbs, nouns, adjectives and mixed methods where the source language is English and the target language is Russian.

Table 6 shows an example of a source sentence in Russian, a reference translation in English and the machine translation sentences in English that have been generated by the NMT models. We can see again that the mixed method has produced more variability in the translation. However, the adverb substitution method also has provided a rich and an accurate translation if we compare it with reference sentence. In general, we can see that the models retrained with augmented data have provided more fluent, accurate and clearer translations than the baseline model.

Method	Translations from Russian to English
Source	Их случай также привлек внимание комиссии по контролю в Женеве.
Reference	Their case also attracted the attention of the control commission in Geneva.
Baseline	**The case** also **brought** to the attention of the Geneva **Monitoring Commission**
Adverbs	The **other case** also **drew** the attention of the **control commission** in Geneva.
Nouns	The case also **attracted** the attention of the **control commission** in Geneva.
Adjectives	The case also **drew** the attention of the **control commission** in Geneva.
Mix	**Others also drew** the attention of the **control commission** in Geneva.

Table 6: Examples of translations obtained when translating using the models trained with the datasets generated using substitution of adverbs, nouns, adjectives and mixed methods where the source language is Russian and the target language is English.

5 Conclusions

In this work, we have automatically generated four new datasets using pre-trained neural language models in order to increase a Russian-English dataset for NMT systems. We have used DA methods by substituting nouns, adjectives and adverbs, or a mix of them observing the importance of selecting the correct type of generated word in order to generate a better-quality sentence.

The generated new datasets have been used for retraining the baseline models in both language directions of translation (from Russian to English and from English to Russian). In addition, the retrained NMT models have been compared performing a quantitative and qualitative analysis showing better results than the baseline models. In conclusion, it is worth noting that the presented DA methods are a viable way of improving NMT systems when there is not enough data or the quality of the data is low. However, there is a lot of work to do in this area in order to improve the method.

In terms of future work, we can also use the verb substitution method which will probably generate richer and broader datasets. However, this method seems to be more complex in terms of quality stability because the number, person and gender (Russian has three types of gender which makes it more complex: feminine, masculine and neutral) must correspond with the rest of the sentence. In addition, we propose the use of a statistic aligner which will significantly reduce the use of machine translation to create synthetic data by only translating a word instead of the full sentence.

References

Bahdanau, D., Cho, K., Montréal, U. D., Bengio, Y., and Montréal, U. D. (2015). Neural machine translation by jointly learning to align and translate. In *3rd International Conference on Learning Representations, ICLR 2015.*

Brown, T. B., Mann, B., Ryder, N., Subbiah, M., Kaplan, J., Dhariwal, P., Neelakantan, A., Shyam, P., Sastry, G., Askell, A., Agarwal, S., Herbert-Voss, A., Krueger, G., Henighan, T., Child, R., Ramesh, A., Ziegler, D. M., Wu, J., Winter, C., Hesse, C., Chen, M., Sigler, E., Litwin, M., Gray, S., Chess, B., Clark, J., Berner, C., McCandlish, S., Radford, A., Sutskever, I., and Amodei, D. (2020). Language models are few-shot learners.

Devlin, J., Chang, M.-W., Lee, K., and Toutanova, K. (2019). Bert: Pre-training of deep bidirectional transformers for language understanding. In *Proceedings of the 2019 Conference of the North American Chapter of the Association for Computational Linguistics: Human Language Technologies, Volume 1 (Long and Short Papers)*, pages 4171–4186.

Doddington, G. (2002). Automatic evaluation of machine translation quality using n-gram co-occurrence statistics. In *Proceedings of the Second International Conference on Human Language Technology Research*, page 138–145.

Fadaee, M., Bisazza, A., and Monz, C. (2017). Data augmentation for low-resource neural machine translation. In *Proceedings of the 55th Annual Meeting of the Association for Computational Linguistics (Volume 2: Short Papers)*, pages 567–573, Vancouver, Canada. Association for Computational Linguistics.

Floridi, L. and Chiriatti, M. (2020). Gpt-3: Its nature, scope, limits, and consequences. *Minds and Machines*, 30:681–694.

Honnibal, M. and Montani, I. (2017). spaCy 2: Natural language understanding with Bloom embeddings, convolutional neural networks and incremental parsing. To appear.

Kumar, V., Choudhary, A., and Cho, E. (2020). Data augmentation using pre-trained transformer models. In *Proceedings of the 2nd Workshop on Life-long Learning for Spoken Language Systems*, pages 18–26.

Papineni, K., Roukos, S., Ward, T., and Zhu, W.-J. (2002). Bleu: a method for automatic evaluation of machine translation. In *Proceedings of the 40th annual meeting of the Association for Computational Linguistics*, pages 311–318.

Perez, L. and Wang, J. (2017). The effectiveness of data augmentation in image classification using deep learning. *Convolutional Neural Networks Vis. Recognit*, 11:1–8.

Popović, M. (2015). chrf: character n-gram f-score for automatic mt evaluation. In *Proceedings of the Tenth Workshop on Statistical Machine Translation*, pages 392–395.

Rei, R., Stewart, C., Farinha, A. C., and Lavie, A. (2020). Comet: A neural framework for mt evaluation. In *Proceedings of the 2020 Conference on Empirical Methods in Natural Language Processing (EMNLP)*, pages 2685–2702.

Sánchez-Cartagena, V. M., Esplà-Gomis, M., Pérez-Ortiz, J. A., and Sánchez-Martínez, F. (2021). Rethinking data augmentation for low-resource neural machine translation: A multi-task learning approach. In *Proceedings of the 2021 Conference on Empirical Methods in Natural Language Processing*, pages 8502–8516, Online and Punta Cana, Dominican Republic. Association for Computational Linguistics.

Sennrich, R., Haddow, B., and Birch, A. (2016). Improving neural machine translation models with monolingual data. In *Proceedings of the 54th Annual Meeting of the Association for Computational Linguistics (Volume 1: Long Papers)*, pages 86–96.

Snover, M., Dorr, B. J., Schwartz, R., Micciulla, L., and Makhoul, J. (2006). A study of translation edit rate with targeted human annotation. *Proceedings of Association for Machine Translation in the Americas*, pages 223–231.

Stanojević, M. and Sima'an, K. (2014). Beer: Better evaluation as ranking. In *Proceedings of the Ninth Workshop on Statistical Machine Translation*, pages 414–419, Baltimore, Maryland, USA.

Vaswani, A., Shazeer, N., Parmar, N., Uszkoreit, J., Jones, L., Gomez, A. N., Kaiser, L., and Polosukhin, I. (2017). Attention is all you need. In *Proceedings of the 31st International Conference on Neural Information Processing Systems*, page 6000–6010.

Wei, J. and Zou, K. (2019). EDA: Easy data augmentation techniques for boosting performance on text classification tasks. In *Proceedings of the 2019 Conference on Empirical Methods in Natural Language Processing and the 9th International Joint Conference on Natural Language Processing (EMNLP-IJCNLP)*, pages 6382–6388.

Yang, Z., Dai, Z., Yang, Y., Carbonell, J., Salakhutdinov, R., and Le, Q. V. (2019). Xlnet: Generalized autoregressive pretraining for language understanding. In *NeurIPS*, volume 32.

Zhuang, L., Wayne, L., Ya, S., and Jun, Z. (2021). A robustly optimized bert pre-training approach with post-training. In *Proceedings of the 20th Chinese National Conference on Computational Linguistics*, pages 1218–1227.

Ziemski, M., Junczys-Dowmunt, M., and Pouliquen, B. (2016). The united nations parallel corpus v1. 0. In *Proceedings of the Tenth International Conference on Language Resources and Evaluation LREC 2016*.

Efficient Machine Translation Corpus Generation

Kamer Ali Yuksel kamer@aixplain.com
Ahmet Gunduz ahmet.gunduz@aixplain.com
Shreyas Sharma shreyas.sharma@aixplain.com
Hassan Sawaf hassan@aixplain.com
aiXplain Inc., 16535 Grant Bishop Lane, Los Gatos, CA 95032, USA

Abstract

This paper proposes an efficient and semi-automated method for human-in-the-loop post-editing for machine translation (MT) corpus generation. The method is based on online training of a custom MT quality estimation metric on-the-fly as linguists perform post-edits. The online estimator is used to prioritize worse hypotheses for post-editing, and auto-close best hypotheses without post-editing. This way, significant improvements can be achieved in the resulting quality of post-edits at a lower cost due to reduced human involvement. The trained estimator can also provide an online sanity check mechanism for post-edits and remove the need for additional linguists to review them or work on the same hypotheses. In this paper, the effect of prioritizing with the proposed method on the resulting MT corpus quality is presented versus scheduling hypotheses randomly. As demonstrated by experiments, the proposed method improves the lifecycle of MT models by focusing the linguist effort on production samples and hypotheses, which matter most for expanding MT corpora to be used for re-training them.

1 Introduction

Improving MT models requires continuously expanding their MT corpora for re-training cycles by post-editing their outputs on samples received from the production environment. Hence, the MT model lifecycle requires continuous human effort, which could scale and be more efficient by semi-automating it via machine-learning models trained by linguists. Those models can be used to select the maximally useful set of translations to store and post-edit by looking at what is challenging for an MT. They can upsample and prioritize translation outputs from where MTs are not performing well, and reduce costs by post-editing production translations intelligently. The continuous and interactive nature of the MT lifecycle provides the perfect ground for applying active-learning techniques in training those machine-learning models for semi-automation. Custom translation quality or post-editing effort estimation models trained on-the-fly as linguists post-edit translations can be used to prioritize samples accumulating from the model inferences in the production environment. The trained estimators enable to focus the linguist effort on the most challenging samples for the MT model requiring the most post-edits, which are also the most valuable to check for evaluating the MT model quality by humans.

In the WMT20 Metrics Shared Task (Mathur et al., 2020), participants were asked to score MT outputs in the WMT20 News Translation Task with automatic metrics, and four referenceless metrics were submitted. Those metrics (OpenKiwi-BERT, OpenKiwi-XLMR, YISI-2, COMET-QE) use bilingual mappings of the contextual embeddings extracted from pre-trained or fine-tuned language models (like XLM-RoBERTa) to evaluate the cross-lingual lexical semantic similarity between the input and MT output. However, it has been seen that those metrics generally struggle to score human translations against machine translations reliably except for COMET-QE (Rei et al., 2020), which was the only reference-free metric that was able to differentiate human translations from MT. Freitag et al. (2021a) carried out an MQM research study by scoring the outputs of top systems from the WMT20 Metrics Shared Task in two language pairs using annotations provided by professional translators with access to the entire document context. Their study shows that crowd-worker human evaluations (as conducted by WMT) have a low correlation with MQM, and the resulting system-level rankings are quite different; and questioned previous conclusions based on crowd-worker human evaluation, especially for high-quality MT. Most importantly, they also found that automatic metrics based on pre-trained embeddings can outperform human crowd workers. This was a clear indication that machine learning models trained over crowd-sourced human-evaluations can reach a higher generalization performance than individual evaluators; thus, they can be used for sanity-checking.

In the WMT21 Metrics Shared Task (Freitag et al., 2021b), contrary to the previous year, they have also acquired their human ratings based on expert-based human evaluation, which has shown to be more reliable, via MQM; and were able to evaluate all metrics on two different domains (news and TED talks) using translations of the same MT systems. It has been found that reference-free metrics (in particular COMET-QE and OpenKiwi) perform very well in scoring human translations but not as well with MT outputs. They are also relatively good at rating human translations at the segment-level while being competitive against their reference-based counterparts in system-level evaluation. REGEMT (Štefánik et al., 2021) was a new reference-free metric of WMT21, which was created as an ensemble of other selected metrics of surface, syntactic and semantic-level similarity as input features to a regression model that estimates a quality assessment. It used the following input features: Source length, Target length, Contextual SCM, Contextual WMD, BERTScore, Prism, and Compositionality. The ensembling can allow customization and continual learning of their quality estimation metrics. cushLEPOR (Han et al., 2021) customized hLEPOR metric by hyper-tuning its weighting-parameters to better agree with professional human evaluations, including on MQM and pSQM scores; and achieved competitive results against quality estimation metrics based on pre-trained neural models measuring cross-lingual lexical semantic similarity, at a much higher cost.

The primary contributions of this paper are three-fold: (1) proposing a new architecture for managing MT model production lifecycle in a cost-efficient and scalable semi-automated way (2) demonstrating the effective use of referenceless metrics for training dataset building (via post-editing), and human evaluation processes of this lifecycle (3) active-learning of custom referenceless metrics as machine learning targets are collected from the human-annotators. To the best of our knowledge, there is no previous work that studies how to employ quality estimation metrics to improve the production lifecycle of MT systems by prioritizing the incoming translations to be evaluated or post-edited. Furthermore, none of the previous work in the literature also studied how custom quality metrics can be trained on-the-fly in an active-learning fashion. Finally, none of them also reported how that would affect the quality of human post-edits by semi-automation at different human-involvement levels. The comparison between random prioritization and the personalized metric is provided in the experiments section, not only by scoring accuracy but also by their effect on reference building by post-editing.

2 Related Work

There have been previous attempts to use active-learning for more efficient corpus extension for MT, but those were using model-free (based on diversity) and (neural MT) model-based uncertainty sampling methods. Peris and Casacuberta (2018) used active-learning for interactive MT where they have selected hypotheses that are worth being supervised by human agents by exploiting the attention mechanism of a neural MT as a measure of uncertainty. Zeng et al. (2019)

used paraphrastic embeddings from unsupervised pre-training to sample diverse sentences for active-learning in MT. They have also proposed an alternative using information-loss during bi-directional translation. Hu and Neubig (2021) also performed uncertainty-based active-learning for fine-tuning MTs by selecting phrases for translation rather than translating entire sentences. In this work, instead of using uncertainty-based proxy-measures for the difficulty of samples for the MT, a reference-free quality-estimator is trained online with MT errors measured by each post-edit. This allows the proposed method not just to select the most challenging sample for post-editing but also to select which hypothesis should be used for post-editing when multiple of them are present. Furthermore, the trained quality estimation model provides a mechanism for sanity-checking or gamifying the post-editing activity of linguists; and also enables augmenting the training corpus by using high-quality hypotheses as pseudo-references for self-training.

3 Methodology

Post-editing should be performed continuously on the translations of MT models in-production for: (1) deciding when an MT model is good enough for deployment, (2) deciding if a new MT is better than its version in-deployment, (3) deciding when a deployed MT model needs to be re-trained, (4) obtaining references to use for re-training MT models with extended corpora. This work aimed to improve and scale all those manual processes for managing the lifecycle of MT models in-production for their continual improvement, evaluation, and debugging. Estimating the difficulty of translations for an MT can be helpful in deciding which of them to post-edit. This way, the manual labor in post-editing can be reduced; while increasing its effectiveness by upsampling challenging translations where the MT is estimated not to perform well.

In this work, MT corpus generation is conducted more effectively by training a machine-learning (ML) model iteratively with each post-edit from the linguists. This ML model is used to efficiently generate MT corpora by prioritizing post-edit efforts of human translators and providing them real-time feedback through model predictions of the post-edits. The ML model can simultaneously be used for performing sanity checks on linguists by checking the discrepancies between each and its own decisions. MT hypotheses that are efficiently and semi-automatically post-edited, can be used as training corpora to re-train or fine-tune MTs, or as validation corpora to benchmark them. Many MT vendors allow their customers to customize their MTs to their application for better performance when a custom corpus is available with references. As a result of selecting and post-editing translations from production systems, one also obtains references necessary to automatically score them with industry-standard MT scoring metrics.

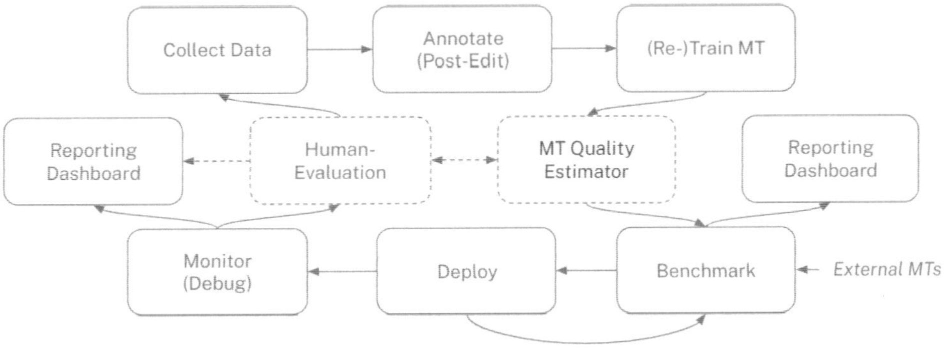

Figure 1: The architecture of the proposed method for efficient MT corpus generation.

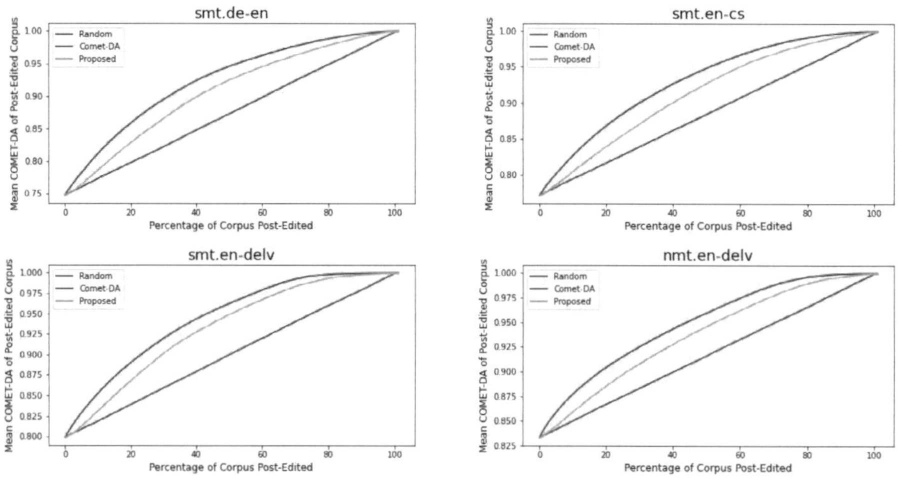

Figure 2: The corpus quality (measured by COMET-DA) achieved when hypotheses are ranked by COMET-DA estimator (yellow), randomly (green), and COMET-DA ground-truth (red).

The architecture of the proposed method is illustrated in Figure 1 where a reference-free custom MT quality estimator, which is trained online by obtained post-edits iteratively, is the central component that drives the continuous post-editing process in MT model production lifecycle efficiently by prioritizing it. The obtained post-edits can be treated as ground-truth references for benchmarking with reference-based scores on translations coming from the deployment, and later for re-training a new version of the MT model that will be shadow-tested against the previous version in-production environment. External MTs can optionally be used in the process not just for comparing against but also for providing alternative translations selected for post-editing when less linguist effort is estimated. They can also enable round-trip translations of source texts for the data-augmentation of training samples for the estimator.

The estimator trained with online AutoML functionalities in FLAML framework (Wang et al., 2021), uses fine-tuned cross-lingual embeddings of COMET-QE score as features, alongside many other linguistic ones extracted with Stanza (Qi et al., 2020) from source texts and their translations: the number of tokens, characters, and the average word length of sentences; the frequency of Part-of-Speech and Named Entity Recognition labels, and the frequency of morphological features. The differences in values of linguistic features and COMET-QE embeddings between source texts and translations, cosine distance of their COMET-QE embeddings, and the pointwise product of COMET-QE embeddings of source texts and their translations are also included as features. When the source or target language is English, an additional 250 linguistic (syntax, semantics, discourse, and readability) features are extracted with LingFeat library (Lee et al., 2021) in SpaCy. COMET-DA (the reference-based version of COMET metric trained on Direct Assessments) and Translation-Error-Rate (TER) metrics in-between MT hypotheses and their respective post-edits are attempted as regression targets, with mean-squared error as the training objective. After the model update on each post-edit, the next sample with the lowest estimated COMET-DA or highest estimated TER is prioritized for the linguist post-editing.

4 Experiments

The QT21 corpus (Specia, 2017), a publicly available dataset containing industry-generated sentences from information technology and life sciences domains, has been used in the experiments. The corpus contained 179K tuples of source and their respective reference sentences for which an MT hypothesis, either from a statistical or a neural MT model, and its post-edit is also provided. Some (43K) of the tuples in the dataset were for German-English (de-en) language-pair; whereas the remaining 136K was translations from English into one of the target languages (Czech, German, Latvian) available. The experiments were conducted for the hypotheses of statistical and neural MTs (SMT and NMT, respectively) individually on four sub-corpora. Table 1 shows the size of each sub-corpus and the performance of the COMET-DA estimator regarding blind predictions collected during online training (before training with each sample). It can be seen that the estimator achieves a high ranking-correlation with the regression target, which demonstrates its capability in prioritizing post-edits regarding how critical they are.

The experimental results are presented for MT quality estimators trained with COMET-DA and TER targets. The estimators trained online with each post-edit are used to re-prioritize the post-editing queue after each learning step. The mean quality or translation error of the corpus is calculated with ground-truth references available and logged after each post-edit. The MT models are not re-trained with generated corpora during the course of post-editing. It has been observed that the proposed method reaches a better corpus quality with fewer post-edits in all of the datasets as shown in the following results. Table 2 and 3 shows the percentage gain of the proposed method on each dataset against ranking randomly in terms of COMET-DA and TER respectively. It can be observed that the mean corpus quality obtains the highest gain (6-8% in inverse-TER) versus ranking randomly when around half of the corpus is post-edited, where the mean TER of the corpus would be lower up to 20% than ranking-randomly for post-editing.

It can be assumed that due to limited resources, only a portion of the whole dataset would be post-edited by linguists in many real-world cases. Based on the demonstrated experimental results, one can conclude that active-learning to schedule post-edits leads to more efficient use of linguists than ranking hypotheses randomly for post-editing. As shown also in Figure 2, the Pareto-optimal corpus quality is achieved when 40-50% of those hypotheses are post-edited by de-prioritizing ones where post-editing would not lead to a significant improvement. The mean corpus quality indicated by COMET-DA already reaches up to 95% when half of the hypotheses are post-edited with up to half error (inverse COMET-DA) than ranking randomly. As the reduction of error is more significant in COMET-DA than in TER, it can be said that humans are less sensitive in their Direct Assessments to MT errors than automatic metrics when the hypothesis quality is already reasonably high. It has also been observed the proposed method contributes more to the corpus quality when prioritizing SMT hypotheses where it achieves higher ranking-correlation despite reaching better regression performance for NMT. This is probably because the qualities of SMT hypotheses are more heterogeneous than NMT.

5 Discussion

Since the proposed method depends on the embeddings from XLM-RoBERTa model, it is limited to 100 languages that the model was pre-trained with. However, the experimental results indicate that the proposed method is able to generalize to the languages (like Czech and Lat-

Sub-corpus	Samples	MAE	MSE	Spearman ρ	Pearson r	Kendall τ
SMT de-en	43000	0.13	0.03	0.53	0.46	0.38
SMT en-cs	43000	0.12	0.02	0.52	0.46	0.36
SMT en-de,lv	46738	0.10	0.02	0.65	0.55	0.46
NMT en-de,lv	46738	0.08	0.01	0.48	0.44	0.34

Table 1: The regression and ranking performance of the online estimator on four sub-corpora.

SMT de-en	20%	Δ	30%	Δ	40%	Δ	50%	Δ	60%	Δ	70%	Δ	80%	Δ
Random	0.80	0.00%	0.82	0.00%	0.85	0.00%	0.87	0.00%	0.90	0.00%	0.92	0.00%	0.95	0.00%
Proposed	0.83	+3.85%	0.87	+5.27%	0.90	**+6.00%**	0.92	+5.92%	0.94	+5.23%	0.96	+4.20%	0.98	+3.09%
SMT en-cs	20%	Δ	30%	Δ	40%	Δ	50%	Δ	60%	Δ	70%	Δ	80%	Δ
Random	0.82	0.00%	0.84	0.00%	0.86	0.00%	0.88	0.00%	0.91	0.00%	0.93	0.00%	0.95	0.00%
Proposed	0.84	+2.78%	0.87	+3.78%	0.90	+4.50%	0.93	**+4.83%**	0.95	+4.79%	0.97	+4.12%	0.98	+3.11%
SMT en-de,lv	20%	Δ	30%	30%	40%	Δ	50%	Δ	60%	Δ	70%	Δ	80%	Δ
Random	0.84	0.00%	0.86	0.00%	0.88	0.00%	0.90	0.00%	0.92	0.00%	0.94	0.00%	0.96	0.00%
Proposed	0.87	+3.44%	0.90	+4.90%	0.93	**+5.47%**	0.95	+5.43%	0.97	+5.19%	0.98	+4.61%	0.99	+3.45%
NMT en-de,lv	20%	Δ	30%	Δ	40%	Δ	50%	Δ	60%	Δ	70%	Δ	80%	Δ
Random	0.87	0.00%	0.88	0.00%	0.90	0.00%	0.92	0.00%	0.93	0.00%	0.95	0.00%	0.97	0.00%
Proposed	0.88	+2.12%	0.91	+2.81%	0.93	+3.14%	0.95	**+3.24%**	0.96	+3.16%	0.98	+2.98%	0.99	+2.47%

Table 2: The mean corpus quality (in COMET-DA) when prioritized by the proposed COMET-DA estimator versus random-prioritization baseline on different percentages of post-editing.

SMT de-en	20%	Δ	30%	Δ	40%	Δ	50%	Δ	60%	Δ	70%	Δ	80%	Δ
Random	60.13	0.00%	64.76	0.00%	69.72	0.00%	74.72	0.00%	79.42	0.00%	85.71	0.00%	89.84	0.00%
Proposed	62.98	4.74%	69.05	6.62%	74.92	7.45%	80.19	7.32%	85.72	**7.94%**	90.43	6.76%	94.21	4.86%
SMT en-cs	20%	Δ	30%	Δ	40%	Δ	50%	Δ	60%	Δ	70%	Δ	80%	Δ
Random	57.03	0.00%	62.36	0.00%	67.70	0.00%	73.05	0.00%	78.38	0.00%	83.72	0.00%	89.11	0.00%
Proposed	59.26	3.90%	65.81	5.53%	71.70	5.90%	77.46	**6.03%**	82.87	5.74%	87.90	4.99%	92.46	3.77%
SMT en-de,lv	20%	Δ	30%	30%	40%	Δ	50%	Δ	60%	Δ	70%	Δ	80%	Δ
Random	60.18	0.00%	65.08	0.00%	70.02	0.00%	74.89	0.00%	79.74	0.00%	84.69	0.00%	89.73	0.00%
Proposed	63.50	5.53%	69.66	7.03%	75.41	7.71%	80.92	**8.05%**	85.61	7.35%	90.10	6.39%	94.24	5.03%
NMT en-de,lv	20%	Δ	30%	Δ	40%	Δ	50%	Δ	60%	Δ	70%	Δ	80%	Δ
Random	61.78	0.00%	60.50	0.00%	71.24	0.00%	75.93	0.00%	80.66	0.00%	86.37	0.00%	90.25	0.00%
Proposed	64.08	3.73%	70.09	5.40%	75.52	6.00%	80.56	**6.09%**	85.20	5.62%	89.51	4.85%	93.54	3.65%

Table 3: The mean corpus quality (measured by 100-TER) when prioritized by the proposed TER estimator versus random-prioritization baseline on various percentages of post-editing.

vian), which have not been employed in the fine-tuning of that encoder for COMET-QE model. The online training with those language-agnostic embeddings helps the estimator in quickly adapting to the unseen languages or training multi-language estimators as it has been done in this work for German and Latvian by providing the target language as an input feature.

Despite the effect of the proposed method on the corpus quality studied in this work, the resulting effect on the MT model performance after re-training is not measured quantitatively and that is planned to be part of future-work; but it can be assumed to also improve with the better corpus quality where the difficult samples for the MT are prioritized to extend its training corpus. Moreover, the effect of augmenting the MT corpus, by using high-quality MT hypotheses for production samples as pseudo-references, on the resulting MT performance should also be studied. In addition, the contribution of MT re-training iterations on further improving the overall MT corpus quality by updating these pseudo-references can also be measured in future-work. Finally, the combination of the proposed method with diversity-based active-learning techniques (especially using extracted embeddings) will also be studied in future-work, and the experiments will also be extended to compare with those uncertainty-based techniques.

6 Conclusion

Efficiently obtaining references for MT corpora continuously accumulated from production is crucial for improving MT models. MT corpus generation is a costly manual process, and its efficiency and scalability can be significantly improved by training an online ML model that prioritizes the post-editing workload of linguists with high accuracy. In this work, it has been shown that the post-editing process can be improved by prioritizing the samples that need it the most - the ones from which MTs would learn most when re-trained with obtained references. It can be expected that prioritizing the most challenging production samples for corpus generation would also lead to better hypotheses on the remaining samples when MTs are re-trained. The trained estimator can also be helpful in sanity-checking the post-editing performance of each linguist online without the need of a reviewer or a duplicated effort of post-editing to create references. It can also be used to give them feedback to gamify their post-editing process. When hypotheses from multiple MTs are present for each source-text, the estimator can also be used to pre-select the best hypothesis to post-edit, and further increase the linguist efficiency. Finally, it can also be used to prioritize the post-edits of linguists for a manual reviewing process.

References

Freitag, M., Foster, G., Grangier, D., Ratnakar, V., Tan, Q., and Macherey, W. (2021a). Experts, errors, and context: A large-scale study of human evaluation for machine translation. *Transactions of the Association for Computational Linguistics*, 9:1460–1474.

Freitag, M., Rei, R., Mathur, N., Lo, C.-k., Stewart, C., Foster, G., Lavie, A., and Bojar, O. (2021b). Results of the wmt21 metrics shared task: Evaluating metrics with expert-based human evaluations on ted and news domain. In *Proceedings of the Sixth Conference on Machine Translation*, pages 733–774.

Han, L., Sorokina, I., Erofeev, G., and Gladkoff, S. (2021). cushlepor: customising hlepor metric using optuna for higher agreement with human judgments or pre-trained language model labse. In *Proceedings of the Sixth Conference on Machine Translation*, pages 1014–1023.

Hu, J. and Neubig, G. (2021). Phrase-level active learning for neural machine translation. *arXiv preprint arXiv:2106.11375*.

Lee, B. W., Jang, Y. S., and Lee, J. (2021). Pushing on text readability assessment: A transformer meets handcrafted linguistic features. In *Proceedings of the 2021 Conference on Empirical Methods in Natural Language Processing*, pages 10669–10686, Online and Punta Cana, Dominican Republic. Association for Computational Linguistics.

Mathur, N., Wei, J., Freitag, M., Ma, Q., and Bojar, O. (2020). Results of the wmt20 metrics shared task. In *Proceedings of the Fifth Conference on Machine Translation*, pages 688–725.

Peris, Á. and Casacuberta, F. (2018). Active learning for interactive neural machine translation of data streams. *arXiv preprint arXiv:1807.11243*.

Qi, P., Zhang, Y., Zhang, Y., Bolton, J., and Manning, C. D. (2020). Stanza: A Python natural language processing toolkit for many human languages. In *Proceedings of the 58th Annual Meeting of the Association for Computational Linguistics: System Demonstrations*.

Rei, R., Stewart, C., Farinha, A. C., and Lavie, A. (2020). Comet: A neural framework for mt evaluation. *arXiv preprint arXiv:2009.09025*.

Specia, L. (2017). QT21 data. LINDAT/CLARIAH-CZ digital library at the Institute of Formal and Applied Linguistics (ÚFAL), Faculty of Mathematics and Physics, Charles University.

Štefánik, M., Novotný, V., and Sojka, P. (2021). Regressive ensemble for machine translation quality evaluation. *arXiv preprint arXiv:2109.07242*.

Wang, C., Wu, Q., Weimer, M., and Zhu, E. (2021). Flaml: a fast and lightweight automl library. *Proceedings of Machine Learning and Systems*, 3:434–447.

Zeng, X., Garg, S., Chatterjee, R., Nallasamy, U., and Paulik, M. (2019). Empirical evaluation of active learning techniques for neural mt. In *Proceedings of the 2nd Workshop on Deep Learning Approaches for Low-Resource NLP (DeepLo 2019)*, pages 84–93.

Building and Analysis of Tamil Lyric Corpus with Semantic Representation

Karthika Ranganathan karthika.cyr@gmail.com
Geetha T V tv_g@hotmail.com
Department of Computer Science and Engineering, Anna University, Chennai, 600025, India

Abstract

In the new era of modern technology, the cloud has become the library for many things including entertainment, i.e, the availability of lyrics. In order to create awareness about the language and to increase the interest in Tamil film lyrics, a computerized electronic format of Tamil lyrics corpus is necessary for mining the lyric documents. In this paper, the Tamil lyric corpus was collected from various books and lyric websites. Here, we also address the challenges faced while building this corpus. A corpus was created with 15286 documents and stored all the lyric information obtained in the XML format. In this paper, we also explained the Universal Networking Language (UNL) semantic representation that helps to represent the document in a language and domain independent ways. We evaluated this corpus by performing simple statistical analysis for characters, words and a few rhetorical effect analysis. We also evaluated our semantic representation with the existing work and the results are very encouraging.

1 Introduction

Tamil (pronounced as Tamizh) is one of the ancient and classical Indian languages spoken in Tamil Nadu. At the beginning of the 21st century, about 66 million people were speaking Tamil language, one of the oldest languages surviving from 300 BCE (Annamalai and Steever, 1998). Some people in Sri Lanka, Malaysia, Singapore, Mauritius, Fiji Islands, Canada and South Africa are also currently speaking Tamil language [1]. According to the history of Tamil grammar and lexical changes, the period can be categorized into three, old Tamil (300 BCE-700 CE, Sangam period), Middle Tamil (700 – 1600) and modern from 1600 (Thomas, 1998). Very few literature exists from the old Tamil containing 2381 poems by 473 poets and about 102 of which remained anonymous (Shinu, 2003).

Scholars from the Sangam period dealt with emotional and material topics such as war, governance and trade. These literatures are difficult to understand and require literates to explain. In the late 19th century, Tamil literature has been simplified so that everyone can understand, which has created interests amongst Tamil people. Poets like Subramaniya Bharathi utilized the power of Tamil language to create awareness of freedom for both women and British India. In the last century, songs in Tamil films have also played a vital role in interacting with people on social and political issues.

In the modern form, Tamil cinema can be classified as a combination of drama and songs, where the latter is composed with music according to a different genre of the lyrics. In the recent past, the encroachment of foreign languages, Tamil film lyrics are mixed with other language words which was a challenging task to build the lyric corpus.

[1] http://salc.uchicago.edu/tamil-at-chicago

Mining lyric documents facilitates the users to get the lyric characteristics, such as emotion, genre and a lyricist and also search the lyrics on the web. The linguistic features are however inadequate for identifying lyric characteristics, especially for morphologically rich languages like Tamil. For extracting higher level features, we chose semantic representation based on Universal Networking Language (UNL), which defines the conceptual structure in the form of a semantic graph [2]. To the best of our knowledge, no work has been done previously to build a Tamil lyric corpus with semantic graph representation.

The rest of the paper is organized as follows. Section 2 describes the related work. In section 3, we discuss the linguistic issues faced while building the Tamil lyric corpus. Section 4 explains about building the Tamil lyric corpus and illustrates some statistics about it. The evaluation of the corpus is given in Section 5. Finally, Section 6 concludes the paper with future work.

2 Related Work

In this section, we discussed related work carried out for the creation of corpus of Tamil and other languages. Shikhar et al. (2012) created a raw corpus for Assamese language. They build the corpus with a total of 1.5 Million words from their main categories such as Media, learned material and literature. In another work, Sarkar et al. (2007) explained the procedure and issues of automatic corpus creation for Bangla language. Vandana and Dash (2018) developed the Newspaper text corpus for Hindi language. They considered 4 online websites of Newspapers with a fixed time span of 10 years (2007-2016) and built a million-word corpus of the Hindi newspaper texts.

The first corpus for Tamil language was created by Technological Development for Indian Languages (TDIL), the Department of Electronics, Govt. of India. This consists of more than 3 million words from various domains (Francis et al., 1995). Later on, various research organizations are working for the improvement and annotated of Central Institute of Indian Languages (CIIL) Tamil corpus (Rajendran, 2006). Rachakonda et al. (2011) developed an annotation corpus of discourse connectives and their arguments by using 2,00,000 sentences of Tamil encyclopedia articles. Tamil Emotional speech corpus was built by Vijesh (2013) and identified five emotions of Happy, Sad, Anger, Fear, and Neural using GMM classifier. Analysis of lyrics based on the usage of words, concepts co-occuring and rhymes has been done by (Ranganathan et al., 2011). The same author has developed the lyric visualization tool to visualize each lyric characteristic such as emotion, genre, rhyming features, pleasantness and rhetorical style based on statistical modelling (Ranganathan et al., 2013). Chinnappa and Dhandapani (2021) built a new Tamil lyric corpus with a dataset of 5449 songs and identified the lyricist of the song using the BERT model. In our corpus, the number of lyrics is high and also the semantic representation is available for the document. This semantic information is useful to translate the Tamil lyric into other natural languages and also to identify the semantic textual similarity (Singh and Bhattacharyya, 2012), relation extraction (Nguyen and Ishizuka, 2006), search engine (Saviya shree et al., 2013) and sentiment analysis (Rani, 2014).

A language independent semantic representation of UNL has been used to convey the word and content based information of the document (Uchida et al., 1999). Parteek Kumar (2012) proposed a UNL based MT system for Punjabi language by developing Punjabi EnConverter, Punjabi DeConverter and a web interface for online EnConversion and DeConversion process. The author addressed the limitations of the Punjabi Machine Translation. To the best of our knowledge, there is no semantic graph representation for Tamil lyric documents. For Tamil language, Sridhar et al. (2016), have proposed the English-Tamil Machine translation system using UNL. They also developed the sentence formation algorithm to rearrange the Tamil words

[2]http://www.undl.org/unlsys/unl/unl2005

into correct sentences. In another work, UNL semantic representation has been developed by (Jagan et al., 2011) for the tourism domain using rule based approach. This work is not suitable for lyric semantic representation, since the relations and the contextual information in the lyric documents are different. Although, several corpora have been developed for Tamil language and non-Tamil languages for different domains, there is not enough corpus size available to perform applications, such as automatic generation of lyrics, lyric similarity, emotion, genre identification or other Natural Language Processing (NLP) related tasks.

3 Linguistic aspects of Traditional and Lyric Documents

From the viewpoint of linguistic criteria, lyric documents have more interesting issues when compared to traditional documents. The processing of lyrics varies from normal text processing. Usually, the document conveys information about a particular topic, whilst lyrics meant to convey emotion and feelings. In the traditional documents, the sentences sometimes follow the standard subject–verb–object (SVO) structure where the subject comes first, the verb second, and the object third, whereas in the lyric documents, either the verb will be followed by a consecutive noun or the verb may not present in the sentence at all. In addition, some lyrics may contain compound words, colloquial words and in some cases numeral words.

Also, the lyric document contains specific properties such as rhyme, meter, freshness and pleasantness to convey emotions and amenable to music. Special attention was given to defining and extracting these features. Rhyme scheme is used as strings for letters, where each line corresponds to the repetition of same syllables. In Tamil lyrics, the internal and external rhyme schemes are presented with three variations, alliteration, rhyme and end-rhyme, known in Tamil literature as (mōṉai) (first two letters are identical for two words in a rhyme), (etukai) (second two letters are identical for two words in a rhyme) and (iyaipu) (last two letters of the two words in a rhyme are identical) (Rajam, 1992). The freshness of the word based on various timelines facilitated to identify the characteristics of the lyrics. Generation of rhythmic pattern by grouping the strong and weak beats together is measured by using the meter score. Moreover, semantic relations between words of the lyric may be similar to those of documents, however, additional context and semantic attributes need to be extracted to convey the lyric characteristics. The need of tackling the above unique features of lyrics require construction of a large corpus and careful categorization is important for computerization.

4 Building Lyric Corpus for Tamil Language

In the recent days, most of the researchers focus on the automatic extracting and processing of lyrics (Rafael et al., 2014). Tamil films consist of several thousand lyrics; however, a huge amount of these lyrics is not yet computerized. Hence, it is very important to build a Tamil film lyric corpus. In this paper, a Tamil lyric corpus has been built by tagging the un-annotated corpus and used to determine the lyric characteristics.

Figure 1 shows the diagram for building a Tamil lyric corpus. For building the lyric corpus, we follow four steps, i) Data collection, ii) Data refinement, iii) Data Tagging and iv) Data validation.

4.1 Data collection

Lyric data are collected from books and websites. A large number of lyrics are downloaded from the Tamil website, such as Thenkinnam [3]. Crawler was used to retrieve the lyrics from the websites. Most of the lyric websites contain the information about the lyrics such as movie name, year and singers and in some cases the lyricist name, composer name. In addition, we have also

[3] http://thenkinnam.blogspot.in/

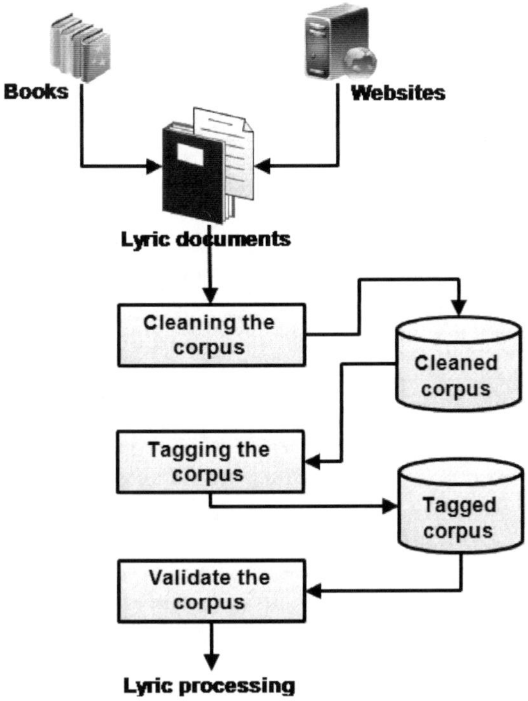

Figure 1: Building a Tamil lyric corpus

collected the Transliterated English documents of Tamil film lyrics. By applying heuristic rules, these documents have been converted into Tamil lyric documents. Only the legendary authors printed books were available to extract the data for Tamil film lyrics. For our corpus creation, we used the books from different lyricists Kannadasan, Vaali and Vairamuthu.

The collections of data were saved as a file with an index number and the title of the song. This helped in avoiding duplication of the songs whilst collecting the lyrics. However, at some instances, there are two different songs with a slight variation in the words of the lyrics. For example, in the Tamil film "7g rainbow colony", a song "நினைத்து நினைத்து பார்த்தேன் – niṉaittu niṉaittu pārttēṉ (I remembered and remembered)" appeared twice with the same title, written by the same author and the music were composed by the same musician. For these types, the entire lyrics of the songs were analysed and the additional information which made it distinct was gathered and stored in the corpus with the emotional tag, happy or sad for identifying the sentiment polarity of the words. This helped in avoiding the elimination of songs with only slight variation in lyric content.

4.2 Data refinement

After collecting freeform data, a substantial cleaning process is required to resolve the linguistic problems such as spelling variations, spelling errors, dialectual variations, foreign langauges encroachment and joined words/lines problems by applying heuristic rules. In addition, single phase lyrics and undefined Universal Character Set Transformation Format (UTF)) characters were filtered out from the data collection.

4.3 Data tagging

The cleaned lyric data are stored in the database. In our work, we used a XML format to store the information obtained from the collected data. This format is mainly used to retrieve the data and also to add or remove the data easily. Normally, in Indian film lyrics including Tamil lyrics, the structure of a lyric is composed of three parts. The first part of the song is called "Pallavi", which represents the theme of the song. "Anupallavi" is the second part, which comes after the "pallavi" and it is optional in most of the cases in lyrics. The final part of the lyric is the "charanam", which has been used to convey the detailed information of the song. Note that in few lyrics more than one charanam is also present. Hence, for each lyric, along with the information obtained, the pallavi, anupallavi and charanam parts are also tagged and represented in the XML format, an exemplar has been shown in Table 1 for a Tamil lyric example:

4.4 Data validation

Validation has been carried out manually by 15 Tamil linguistic experts in the Tamil Computing Lab (TaCoLa lab - Anna University, India) and the statistics of the data cleaned is shown in Table 2 and lyric corpus set is shown in Table 3.

This corpus has been used in many of lyric processing techniques. The main focus is on Tamil film lyric mining since the existence of numerous Tamil songs and the availability of Tamil lyrics available on the web makes this mining an interesting issue. Understanding lyrics and identification of lyric characteristics, from the lyric data set are challenging issues.

4.5 Semantic representation - UNL

The semantic processing of any natural language is represented using Universal Networking Language (UNL), which helps to construct the semantic graph for each sentence as a hypergraph, in which the nodes represent the universal words (concept) and the link represent the relations (exist between concepts). UNL consists of three components, namely, Universal Words (UWs) – representing the meaning of a word or a sentence, UNL relations – representing the relationship between two different concepts in a sentence, and UNL attributes – representing the mood, tense, aspect, etc. (Uchida et al., 1999).

A UW is made up of a character string as head word (an English-language word) followed by a list of constraints. The headword is an English word that is interpreted as a label for a set of concepts. However, the constraints list restricts the interpretation of a UW to a specific concept included within the basics of UW and a set of 58 semantic relations that connects two different UWs within a sentence. An exemplar of a lyric sentence and its semantic representation is shown in Figure 2.

Example: நான் மலரோடு தனியாக ஏன் இங்கு நின்றேன் - Nāṉ malarōṭu taṉiyāka ēṉ iṅku niṉṟēṉ (Why am I standing here alone with the flower)

Figure 2 shows the UNL semantic constraints, UNL relations and UNL attributes used for the example lyric line. Here, icl>person, agt>thing, pof>plant, aoj>thing and icl>place indicate the semantic constraints, which helps to identify whether the concept is a person, or place, or object, etc. @verb represents the UNL attributes and man, obj, agt and plc represents semantic relations between the two concepts.

5 Evaluation

5.1 Analysis of corpus

We present a detailed analysis of our Tamil lyric corpus. This analysis has been used in the lyric search engine and lyric processing tasks, namely, emotion, genre, lyricist, and similarity of lyrics. For lyric analysis, we used frequency occurrence of character and word usage. Also, the usage of rhetorical effects such as metaphor and simile in the corpus has been identified. In

No	Description	Example
1	Title of the lyric	<தலைப்பு> என்னுயிரே என்னுயிரே </தலைப்பு> <Title> oh my heart </Title> <Talaippu> eṉṉuyirē eṉṉuyirē </talaippu>
2	Name of the movie	<படம்> உயிரே</படம்> <Paṭam> uyirē </paṭam> <Movie name> Soul </Movie name>
3	Composer name for the lyric	<இசை>A.R. ரஹ்மான் </இசை> <Icai>A.R. Rahmāṉ </icai> <Composer> A.R.Rahman </Composer>
4	Lyricist name for the lyric	<வரிகள்> வைரமுத்து </வரிகள்> <Varikaḷ> vairamuttu </varikaḷ> <Lyricist> Vairamuthu </Lyricist>
5	Singer name for the lyric	<பாடியவர்> - </பாடியவர்> <Pāṭiyavar> - </pāṭiyavar> <Snger> - </Singer>
6	Tune name of the lyric	<ராகம்> - </ராகம்> <Rākam> - </rākam> <Tune> - </Tune>
7	Rhythm name of the lyric	<தாளம்> - </தாளம்> <Tāḷam> - </tāḷam> <Rhythm> - </Rhythm>
8	Year of the lyric	<வருடம்>1998</வருடம்> <Varuṭam>1998</varuṭam> <Year> 1998 </Year>
9	Opening or first unit of the lyric	<பல்லவி> என்னுயிரே என்னுயிரே etc. </பல்லவி> <Pallavi> eṉṉuyirē eṉṉuyirē etc </Pallavi> <First unit> Oh my heart ! etc. </First unit>
10	Second unit of the lyric	<அனுபல்லவி> நம் காதலிலே வரும் etc.</அனுபல்லவி> <Aṉupallavi> nam kātalilē varum etc.</Aṉupallavi> <Second unit> We enlight the world etc. </Second unit>
11	Third unit of the lyric	<சரணம்-1> கைகள் நான்கும் etc. </சரணம் - 1> <Caraṇam-1> kaikaḷ nāṉkum etc. </Caraṇam - 1> <Third unit – 1> before intimate etc. </Third unit -1> <சரணம்-2> என்னுயிரே என்னுயிரே etc. </சரணம் - 2> <Caraṇam-2> eṉṉuyirē eṉṉuyirē etc. </Caraṇam - 2> <Third unit – 2> Oh My heart! etc. </Third unit -2>

Table 1: Lyric Tagging

Lyric Corpus	Statistics
Total songs before clean-up	15394
Duplicate (deleted)	64
Single – phrase lyric (deleted)	10
Undefined UTF characters (deleted)	34
Total songs after clean-up	15286

Table 2: Data Clean up Statistics

Lyric Corpus	Statistics
Documents	15286
Lines	212004
Words	917185

Table 3: Lyric corpus set statistics

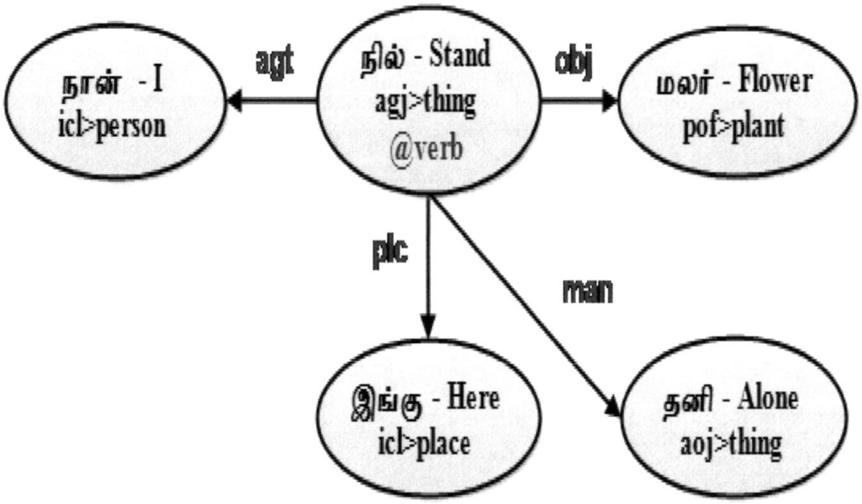

Figure 2: Semantic representation of Tamil lyric sentence

the figurative language, metaphor and simile reveal the feelings of the people strongly. These effects conveyed the meaning of the lyric with a minimal set of words.

5.1.1 Statistical analysis of corpus

Table 4 shows the Top 5 list of frequency distribution of character for Tamil corpus. In Tamil lyric, the least frequently occurred letter was vowel consonant ளௌ and the most frequently occurred letter was a consonant க்.

Table 5 shows the Top 5 list of frequency words from the corpus without function words. Here, we are considering the concept of each word as additional count. For example, the word மலர் – flower has concepts புஷ்பம், மாமலர், பூ and அலரி.

In addition, a large number of lyric documents usually contain many compound and colloquial words (Lestari, 2019). By using (Umamaheswari et al., 2011), we have identified 2528 compound words and 317 colloquial words from the lyric corpus.

Character	Percentage (%)
க் - k	3.28
ப் - p	2.95
த் - t	2.56
ல் - l	2.43
ட் - ṭ	2.16

Table 4: Top 5 frequency characters

Words	Percentage (%)
காதல் - kātal (Love)	2.84
கண் - kaṇ (Eye)	2.19
பூ - pū (Flower)	1.93
நிலவு - Nilavu (Moon)	1.84
மனம் - Maṉam (Mind)	1.68

Table 5: Top 5 frequency words

No	Metaphor	Simile
1	மலர்ப்பாதம் Malarppātam Flower foot	மீன் போன்ற கண்கள் mīṉ pōṉṟa kaṇkaḷ Eyes like fish
2	ரோஜாப்பூ கன்னம் rōjāppū kaṉṉam Rosy cheeks	குயில் போல பாடு kuyil pōla pāṭu Sing like Quail
3	மான்விழி māṉviḻi Deer eye	வில் போன்ற புருவம் vil pōṉṟa puruvam Bow like eyebrow
4	பூவிதழ் pūvitaḻ Flower lips	நிலவை போன்ற முகம் nilavai pōṉṟa mukam Moon like face
5	அன்னநடை aṉṉanaṭai Swan walk	பூ போன்ற முகம் pū pōṉṟa mukam Flower like face

Table 6: Top 5 list of Metaphor and Simile

5.1.2 Rhetorical effect analysis of corpus

Table 6 shows the Top 5 list of metaphor and simile used in the lyric corpus. Here, the metaphors present in the lyric documents are generally in the form of noun-noun and verb-noun compounds. Most lyricists used cue words such as போன்ற - pōṉṟa (like) and போல - pōla (like) for comparisons.

5.2 Comparison of the lyric semantic graph with existing work

From Table 7, our approach results in a high F-measure compared to the rule-based approach (Jagan et al., 2011).

In some cases, lyrics do not always have a verb and therefore the existing work does not form complete semantic graphs. Here, the relations and the contextual information of the documents are different.

Approach	F-measure
Our system	0.61
Existing system	0.52

Table 7: Comparison of our system with existing system

6 Conclusion and Future Work

In this paper, we described the Tamil lyric corpus and the linguistic issues faced during the process. This corpus has been stored in the XML format to add or remove the data easily. We believe that this is the first attempt in creating the Tamil lyric corpus. This paper also discussed the semantic representation for extracting the context level information from the documents. We carried out the evaluation by performing statistical and rhetorical analysis of lyric corpus which resulted in promising results.

In future, we have planned to increase the corpus size of the lyric documents by crawling in the web and annotating various lyric characteristics of emotion, genre, lyricist inferred based on the semantic features. We have also planned to build the semantic representation using a semi-supervised approach. We also planned to extend our work to other morphologically rich languages.

References

Annamalai and Steever, S. B. (1998). *Modern Tamil:The Dravidian Languages*. Taylor and Francis.

Chinnappa, D. and Dhandapani, P. (2021). Tamil Lyrics Corpus: Analysis and Experiments. In *Proceedings of the First Workshop on Speech and Language Technologies for Dravidian Languages*, pages 1–9, Kyiv.

Francis, E., D, J. B., and Ganesan (1995). *Final Report Development of Corpora of Texts of Indian Languages in Machine Readable Form, Part II (Tamil, Telugu, Kannada, Malayalam)*. CIIL.

Jagan, B., Geetha, T. V., Parthasarathi, R., and Karky, M. (2011). Morpho-Semantic Features for Rule- based Tamil Enconversion. *International Journal of Computer Applications (IJCA)*, 26(6):11–18.

Kumar, P. (2012). *UNL-based machine translation system for Punjabi language*. Ph.D thesis, Thapar Institute of Engineering and Technology.

Lestari, F. D. (2019). *An Analysis of Compound Word in the Selected Song Album of Taylor Swift*. Ph.D thesis, STKIP PGRI SIDOARJO.

Nguyen, P. and Ishizuka, M. (2006). A statistical approach for Universal Networking Language-based relation extraction. In *Proceedings of the International Conference on Research, Innovation and Vision for the Future*, pages 153–160, Ho Chi Minh City, Vietnam.

Rachakonda, Teja, R., and Sharma, D. M. (2011). Creating an annotated tamil corpus as a discourse resource. In *Proceedings of the 5th Linguistic Annotation Workshop*, pages 119–123, Portland, Oregon, USA.

Rafael, R., Almeida, M. A., and Carlos, N. S. J. (2014). The ethnic lyrics fetcher tool. *EURASIP Journal on Audio, Speech, and Music Processing*, 27(1):1–10.

Rajam, V. (1992). *A Reference Grammar of Classical Tamil Poetry*. American philosophical society.

Rajendran, S. (2006). *A Survey of the state of the art in Tamil language technology*. Language in India.

Ranganathan, K., Barani, B., and Geetha, T. V. (2013). A Tamil lyrics search and visualization system. *Lecture Notes in Computer Science*, 8281(1):513–527.

Ranganathan, K., Geetha, T. V., Parthasarathi, R., and Karky, M. (2011). Lyric mining Word, rhyme and concept co-occurrence analysis. In *Proceedings of the Tamil Internet Conference*, pages 276–281, Philadelphia, USA.

Rani, S. (2014). *Rule Based Sentiment Analysis System*. Ph.D thesis, THAPAR UNIVERSITY.

Sarkar, A. I., Shahriar, D., Pavel, H., and Khan, M. (2007). *Automatic Bangla corpus creation*. PAN Localization Working Papers.

Saviya shree, K. V., Umamaheswari, E., Jagan, B., Geetha, T. V., and Parthasarathi, R. (2013). Concept Based Search Engine (CBSE) System for Tamil and English. In *Proceedings of the International Tamil Internet Conference*, pages 105–111, University Of Malaya, Kuala Lumpur, Malaysia.

Shikhar, S., Bharali, H., Deka, A. G. R., and Barman, A. (2012). A structured approach for building assamese corpus: insights, applications and challenges. In *Proceedings of the 10th Workshop on Asian Language Resources*, pages 21–28, Mumbai, India.

Shinu, A. (2003). Chera, chola, pandya: Using archaeological evidence to identify the tamil kingdoms of early historic south india. *Asian Perspectives*, 42:207 – 223.

Singh, J.and Bhattacharya, A. and Bhattacharyya, P. (2012). janardhan: Semantic textual similarity using universal networking language graph matching. In *Proceedings of the First Joint Conference on Lexical and Computational Semantics (SEM)*, pages 662–666, Montreal, Canada.

Sridhar, R., Sethuraman, and Krishnakumar (2016). English to Tamil machine translation system using universal networking language. *Sādhanā*, 41(1):607–620.

Thomas, L. (1998). *Old Tamil:The Dravidian Languages*. Taylor and Francis.

Uchida, H., Zhu, M., and Senta, T. (1999). *A gift for a millennium*. The United Nations University.

Umamaheswari, E., Ranganathan, K., T V Geetha, Parthasarathi, R., and Karky, M. (2011). Enhancement of Morphological analyzer with compound, numeral and colloquial word handler. In *Proceedings of the 9th International Conference on Natural Language Processing*, pages 177–186, Anna University, Chennai, India.

Vandana and Dash, N. S. (2018). *Creation and Compilation of Hindi Newspaper Text Corpus*. Language in India.

Vijesh, J. C. (2013). Building and evaluation of tamil emotional speech corpus. In *Proceedings of the 5th National Conference on Signal Processing Communication and VLSI Design*, pages 389–392, Coimbatore, Tamil Nadu, India.

Ukrainian-To-English Folktale Corpus: Parallel Corpora Creation and Augmentation for Machine Translation in Low-Resource Languages

Olena Burda-Lassen, Ph.D. oburdalassen@gmail.com
Independent Scholar, Colorado, United States

Abstract

Folktales are linguistically very rich and culturally significant in understanding the source language. Historically, only human translation has been used for translating folklore. Therefore, the number of translated texts is very sparse, which limits access to knowledge about cultural traditions and customs. We have created a new Ukrainian-To-English parallel corpus of familiar Ukrainian folktales based on available English translations and suggested several new ones. We offer a combined domain-specific approach to building and augmenting this corpus, considering the nature of the domain and differences in the purpose of human versus machine translation. Our corpus is word and sentence-aligned, allowing for the best curation of meaning, specifically tailored for use as training data for machine translation models.

1. Introduction

Machine translation has tremendous potential in connecting people and cultures. The Ukrainian language has an extensive collection of myths, legends, proverbs, songs, and folktales. They all represent the emotions, beliefs, and world views of Ukrainians.

In this paper, we focus on several widely known Ukrainian folktales, all of which are anonymous due to the nature of this genre. Furthermore, folktales are usually passed on from one generation to another, going back hundreds of years.

Interestingly, many available translations are rather transcreations, in which stories are retold and adapted to the target language and culture. We believe machine translation can be a useful supplemental tool in translating Ukrainian folklore, creating opportunities for more research and knowledge transfer about the Ukrainian language and culture. The first step in improving the machine translation performance of Ukrainian folktales is the creation of a high-quality corpus that addresses domain-specific nuances and challenges.

2. Parallel Corpus Creation and Augmentation

2.1. Available Resources Overview

Historically, Ukrainian has been considered a low-resource language with limited corpora resources (Grabar et al., 2018). However, the creation of WikiMatrix (Schwenk et al., 2021a) and CCMatrix (Schwenk et al., 2021b) has significantly improved access to training data for the Ukrainian language. Even when the size of the parallel corpus is significant, the smaller high-quality corpus can increase translation performance (Yıldız et al., 2014), especially within such a unique and challenging domain.

Therefore, we focused on carefully selecting familiar Ukrainian folktales available in English. One of the most extensive collections of English translations of Ukrainian fairytales and folktales is Project Gutenberg's *Cossack Fairy Tales and Folk Tales*[1]. This collection was initially published in 1894 and was edited and translated by Robert Nisbet Bain[2].

We were looking for available original Ukrainian texts containing culture-loaded words and word combinations (primarily from mythology and social life), which helped in the final decision about selecting respective English translations. In our future work, we will expand the available corpus to include more source and target texts.

Ukrainian original versions of selected folktales come from an online collection of stories for children[3] and blogs about Ukrainian traditions[4]. English translations are used from the Gutenberg Project and available translations of folktales[5].

We created this corpus to support a narrow domain of Ukrainian folklore. However, it could also work for the general translation of informational texts about Ukrainian culture. Recently, interest in the Ukrainian language and cultural knowledge has risen. We have found a website containing information about Ukrainian traditions, including many familiar folktales, legends, song lyrics, and stories about customs and holidays. This website is written in Ukrainian and is recommended for English speakers to read in its machine-translated version[6]. It is an excellent example of a practical machine translation application.

Unfortunately, only a limited number of folktales are translated into English. Machine translation models trained using the proposed corpus could fill this gap and help spread knowledge about the Ukrainian language and culture.

2.2. Methods

Our corpus consists of Ukrainian and English versions of 4 popular folktales: "The Mitten," "The Straw Ox," "The Bully Goat," and "Oh: The Tsar of the Forest."

The total number of aligned pairs of sentences and words is 400: the number of English words is 6,800, and the number of Ukrainian words is 4,157. This corpus is the start of our new project, and the number of parallel texts will be increasing consistently.

We have reviewed several available English versions of a well-known folktale, *The Mitten*[7], retold by Jan Brett, as well as *The Mitten: An Old Ukrainian Folktale*[8], by Alvin Tresselt, and decided to include our own, more literal version of the translation of this folktale.

While available English translations are poetic and commonly accepted in the target language space, we have proposed a more semantic translation instead of its adaptation. To be used as training data for machine translation models, source and target sentences must be translated as accurately as possible.

Due to the nature of this research, we needed to do a substantial amount of manual work related to curating training data.

---

[1] https://www.gutenberg.org/cache/epub/29672/pg29672.txt
[2] https://publicdomainreview.org/collection/cossack-fairy-tales-1916
[3] https://kazky.org.ua/
[4] https://carterhaughschool.com/the-fairy-tales-of-ukraine/
[5] https://pdfslide.net/documents/a-ukrainian-folk-tale-the-bully-goat-.html
[6] https://traditions-in-ua.translate.goog/?_x_tr_sl=uk&_x_tr_tl=en&_x_tr_hl=en&_x_tr_pto=sc
[7] https://janbrett.com/bookstores/mitten_book.htm
[8] Alvin Tresselt. 1964. The mitten: an old Ukrainian folktale. New York: Lothrop, Lee & Shepard Co., Inc.

After manually selecting each sentence in the source language and reviewing the equivalent in the target language, we have compiled sentence pairs. In some cases, source sentences and target language translations contained more or fewer sentences and were out of order or lossy. Therefore, we have aligned them according to the source language (for example, if one Ukrainian sentence was translated into two English sentences, we aligned them by the Ukrainian sentence). The English language column appears first in the corpus for easier corpus access and review by English speakers.

We have also aligned corpus by words to finetune the domain knowledge transfer. The examples we have selected were extracted from the corpus sentences and are culture-loaded words and word combinations, describing food, mythological creatures, and animals, for example, *мед-вино* ("med-vyno": "beer and mead"), *Мавка* ("Mavka": "Mavka, the forest spirit"), and *вовчик-братик* ("vovchyk-bratyk": "brother-wolf").

2.3. Findings

We believe that the success and accuracy of the machine translation system depend on the high accuracy of the rarely used source words. While most common phrases are already being translated accurately by available machine translation engines, it is the rare or cultural terms that get missed or misinterpreted by these engines. Adding an extra layer of culturally significant information can only improve the outcome of the translation process.

In the folktale "The Mitten," there are several proper names of animals consisting of their names and characteristic behavior traits, for example, *Мишка-шкряботушка* ("Myshka-shkryabotushka"). Therefore, we have proposed the translation "Scratching Mouse." The literal meaning of it is "the mouse that scratches on things." Hence, the term "Scratching Mouse," in our opinion, is semantically and stylistically more fitting for machine translation models.

A similar example of another hyphenated compound word from the story "The Mitten" is *Ведмідь-набрідь* ("Vedmid-nabrid"). Again, we suggest translating it to "Bear, the Wanderer." Both of these examples use loan translation with an element of expansion, which serves the informative purpose of corpus creation, tailored explicitly for machine translation systems.

In our corpus, we have also included translations of the words mentioned above by another translator Iryna Zheleznova[9]: "Crunch-Munch the Mouse" and "Grumbly-Rumbly the Bear." These terms work well for the English translation of this folktale in children's literature. It is rhymed and catchy, reflecting the target text's desired presentation.

Another example of an aligned word pair illustrates various translation methods of culture-loaded terms: *Мавка* ("Mavka"), one of the most widely known spirits in Ukrainian mythology. Mavka is a female forest spirit.

We have encountered the following translations of this mythology term: "Mavka" (transliteration), "water-nixie" and "nixie" (adaptation and generalization). Therefore, we propose using transliteration plus expansion to incorporate essential knowledge about this mythological creature: "Mavka, the forest spirit."

We have replaced archaic personal pronouns *thou, thee, thy, thine,* and *ye*, found in the English translation, with equivalent modern English pronouns. The source text does not include archaic pronouns, so we decided to omit their use in the corpus.

We hope that applying these augmentation techniques will further increase the quality of this parallel corpus. Furthermore, numerous examples of domain-specific translations can help train the machine translation model and increase accuracy, especially since examples are carefully curated and hand-picked.

---

[9] https://storytellingforeveryone.net/tag/cumulative-story/

3. Conclusions

Further research is necessary to create more extensive corpora, which we plan to conduct since only a very sparse number of corpora is available in the Ukrainian folktale domain.

However, contrary to the human translation methodology of folklore, machine translation techniques are more literal and descriptive.

We have aligned language pairs by sentences and words during parallel corpus creation to increase training data accuracy. We have observed a need for a significant difference between human and machine translation techniques within the folktale domain.

Ukrainian-To-English Folktale Corpus is publicly available online[10]. We also plan on researching the performance of this corpus on several machine translation models in the future.

References

Genzel Dmitriy, Jakob Uszkoreit, and Franz Och. 2010. “Poetic” Statistical Machine Translation: Rhyme and Meter. In *Proceedings of the 2010 Conference on Empirical Methods in Natural Language Processing*, pages 158–166, Cambridge, MA. Association for Computational Linguistics.

Grabar Natalia, Olga Kanishcheva, Thierry Hamon. Multilingual aligned corpus with Ukrainian as the target language. *SLAVICORP*, Sep 2018, Prague, Czech Republic. ffhalshs-01968343f

Sánchez-Cartagena Víctor M., Miquel Esplà-Gomis, Juan Antonio Pérez-Ortiz, and Felipe Sánchez-Martínez. 2021. Rethinking Data Augmentation for Low-Resource Neural Machine Translation: A Multi-Task Learning Approach. In *Proceedings of the 2021 Conference on Empirical Methods in Natural Language Processing*, pages 8502–8516, Online and Punta Cana, Dominican Republic. Association for Computational Linguistics.

Schwenk Holger, Vishrav Chaudhary, Shuo Sun, Hongyu Gong, and Francisco Guzmán. 2021. WikiMatrix: Mining 135M Parallel Sentences in 1620 Language Pairs from Wikipedia. In *Proceedings of the 16th Conference of the European Chapter of the Association for Computational Linguistics:* Main Volume, pages 1351–1361, Online. Association for Computational Linguistics.

Schwenk Holger, Guillaume Wenzek, Sergey Edunov, Edouard Grave, Armand Joulin, and Angela Fan. 2021. CCMatrix: Mining Billions of High-Quality Parallel Sentences on the Web. In *Proceedings of the 59th Annual Meeting of the Association for Computational Linguistics and the 11th International Joint Conference on Natural Language Processing* (Volume 1: Long Papers), pages 6490–6500, Online. Association for Computational Linguistics.

Yıldız, Eray & Tantuğ, Ahmet & Diri, Banu. (2014). The Effect of Parallel Corpus Quality vs Size in English-To-Turkish SMT. *Computer Science & Information Technology*. 4. 21-30. 10.5121/csit.2014.4710.

[10] https://github.com/Ukrainian-To-English-Corpora/Folktale_corpus

Association for Computational Linguistics
209 N. Eighth Street
Stroudsburg, Pennsylvania 18360

ISBN 978-1-7138-6759-3

CURRAN ASSOCIATES INC.
proceedings.com

International Conference on e-Learning 2018

Held at the Multi-Conference on Computer Science and Information Systems (MCCSIS 2018)

Madrid, Spain
17 – 20 July 2018

iadis